THE EMERGE

"Young Prophets Shall Prophesy"

Weshaun Warren

It is our prayer and declaration that you would maintain a Spirit of Integrity concerning the knowledge shared with you in this manual. Meaning, when using the information in this book publicly, you would give author proper recognition and acknowledgement for the knowledge, work, experience, research, and labor of development of this book.

Thank You In Advance
for your countenance of righteousness and obedience.

ECCLESIASTES 12:14

For God shall bring every work into judgment, with every secret thing, whether it be good, or whether it be evil.

First Edition: 2019

ISBN: 978-1-934905-00-5

Worldwide Kingdom Publishing
1911 Horger St.
Lincoln Park, Michigan 48146

PREFACE

The lack of young people in churches today has increased tremendously over the last decade. The spirit of distraction and fear has caused many young people to flee away from the Body of Christ. The enemy's goal is to get young people off their God-given purpose, especially in the Kingdom of God. He is being smart and strategic now, covering himself in many different ways trying to deceive. This is because we are living in the end times, which the Bible talks about in **2 Timothy 3:1-5**. Telling us about many different events that will occur, reminding us that we are in the end-time. It is time for the next generation to stand and learn as much as we can, so we can have the necessary tools to defeat the enemy. In reading this book for young prophets, you will be ignited to answer the call of the prophetic. The next generation of prophets is so important now, because we will be the ones who will speak what God is saying into the earth. The enemy doesn't want that to happen, so it is imperative that we are in tune with the spiritual side of who we are. In this book, there are tools that will teach you the basic functions and operations of the prophetic realm. You will gain more insight on how to hear God's voice in clarity, what hinders our gifting, and how to know if you are called to be a prophet. It is my prayer that you will not become distracted by your everyday life, but set aside time to gain more intimacy with God. I pray God's grace upon you as you continue your assignment as a prophetic vessel in the earth.

DEDICATION PAGE

This book is dedicated to young people all across the nation, who have the desire to know more about the prophetic call on their life; or those who simply don't know what it means to walk in the prophetic realm. It is my prayer that you will gain new understanding and prophetic insight of the operation and functions of the prophetic. I pray that you will begin to receive a new level of clarity in hearing the voice of God. That you may begin to be stirred up with the fire of God, causing the gifts on the inside of you to come alive! This book will give you a new revelation of what it means to be a young prophet in operation in the Kingdom of God.

I also dedicate this book to those young people, who may feel like there is more to God, then what they are experiencing. Even those who do not know if they are called to this walk in the kingdom. I challenge you to take your place, rightfully in the Kingdom of God.

SPECIAL THANKS

First, I would like to thank my Lord and Savior Jesus Christ, who has entrusted me with such great assignments. I am completely humbled to be an End-time prophetic vessel.

I would also like to thank Apostle Charissee, who has birthed me in the Spirit. Your hard work of labor and sacrifices in prayer are not in vain.

To my parents Pastors Wes & Shauntae Warren, who have helped cultivate my gift and who raised me naturally. Without you guys, I would not be here. Thank you guys for believing in me, even though at times I was disobedient. Also, I can never leave out my fabulous siblings, who have always been my number one supporters.

Then to a good friend who has helped me with the hard work and labor of this book and who has pushed me to finish. I appreciate you, Genesis Maple.

Lastly, to all of my family, church family, and friends who have prayed and interceded for me during this assignment. I really appreciate you all and love you all dearly.

ACCOUNTABILTY PAGE

Unless indicated in footnotes, all scripture references, and quotations are written from the King James Version of the Bible.

It is our prayer and declaration that you would maintain a Spirit of Integrity concerning the knowledge shared with you in this book. Meaning when using the information in this book publicly, you would give author proper recognition and acknowledgement for the knowledge, work, experience, research, and labor of development of this book.

No part of this book may be reproduced by mimeograph process or by another method of duplication unless expressed written has been granted by Weshaun Warren.

Thank you in advance for your countenance of righteousness and obedience.

Ecclesiastes 12:14

For God shall bring every work into judgment, with every secret thing, whether it be good, or whether it be evil.

FORWARD

I am so excited to write this forward for "Emerge" a book for young prophets and those who are interested in prophetic ministry. It is inspiring to see the young prophets go forth in their gifts in the spirit of excellence. This is worthy of great acknowledgement. I have watched Prophet Weshaun develop and mature in his prophetic gifts from a young child. He is definitely a true prophet of God, who operates in a strong prophetic, healing, and deliverance mantle. He is a prophet of order with an Apostolic anointing upon his life.

This book is awesomely, exciting for anyone with a prophetic call, it does not matter about your chronological age nor the number of years you have been saved; you will learn new revelation about the realm of the prophetic. Prophet Weshaun will inspire and ignite you in your prophetic gifts as you receive impartation from the anointing that transfers from reading this book! Get ready to "Emerge" in your prophetic gifts!

In His Service,

Dr. Charissee Lewis

TABLE OF CONTENTS

Part 1- Understanding the Call of the Prophetic

Part 2- The Ministry of the Prophet

PART 1

UNDERSTANDING THE CALL OF THE PROPHETIC

Chapter 1

THE CALL TO THE PROPHETIC

As young people, it is important that we begin to answer our call. **Jeremiah 1:5** says "Before I formed thee in the belly I knew thee, and before thou camest forth out of the womb I sanctified thee, and I ordained thee a prophet unto the nations." Before we were formed God knew us and even before we came out of the womb He has called us to prophesy to the nations. Therefore, it doesn't matter your age or if you feel worthy or not; You are called by God!

A lot of times as young people, we may feel that we are not capable or worthy of the call that is on our lives. We push our gifts to the side, putting God on the shelf until we need Him.

Romans 12:6

We have different gifts according to the grace given to us. If man's gift is prophesying, let him use it in portion of his faith.

Prophecy is a God given gift, in other words, man cannot give this gift nor take it away. This is because there is a grace that is given to the prophetic vessels.

2 Peter 1:21

For prophecy never had its origin in the will of man, but

men spoke from God as they were carried along by the Holy Spirit.

The prophetic realm is a foundational ministry gift. It is present today to help establish structure and a solid base concerning our Lord and Savior.

Prophecy is the vocal gift that God gives man. It is words directly spoken from the heart of God. It is for a specific time, place or person. It's a Rhema "Right Now" word. Prophecy comes to edify, exhort and comfort.

1 Corinthians 14:3

But he that prophecies speaketh unto men to edification, and exhortation, and comfort.

Prophecy is meant to build you up, stir you up and cheer you up, even while being corrected. Why? Because it compels you to draw closer to God, even when dark areas in your life are brought to light. It is a direct channel in which God speaks to man.

Prophesying- is an utterance, fore-tell, and forth-tell; speaking forth the oracles of God.

Utterance- is the action of speaking something aloud.

Fore-telling- is declaring a future blessing or judgement (prediction) to make known beforehand.

Forth-telling- is directly speaking the oracles of God concerning a current situation. This involves comfort, exhortation and edification.

Numbers 11:25

And the Lord came down in a cloud, and spake unto him, and took of the spirit that was upon him, and gave it unto the seventy elders: and it came to pass, that, when the spirit rested upon them, they prophesied, and did not cease.

Matthew 22:14 says that "For many are called, but few are chosen." If you are reading this, I believe that you have been called and chosen for this very mandate. As a young child, I would often preach to my stuffed animals or even the couches. I would then begin to see things and sense things in the Spirit. I would have vivid dreams, see angels, and sometimes I would even see words on people like depression, anger, hurt, etc. I would be able to sense atmospheres and discern situations. God would reveal a strategy on how to move forward or reveal revelatory knowledge of the outcome. I never really understood why this would happen to me or even the meaning of everything I would see and sense around me. I often would love being alone, or it would naturally happen even if I had desired otherwise. Well, I won't say alone but separated. Many people did not understand my mindset, actions and heart causing me to feel alone or like I was weird. On top of that, I had a sharp tongue causing me to communicate, not disrespectfully, but sternly to my parents. These may be some early signs of the prophetic call on your life.

As I got older, I began to hold things inside and this would give the enemy leverage to make me feel alone and unwanted. The enemy even used tactics and temptations of lust and pride to entrap me in the kingdom of darkness. He would try telling me that I was okay and that I did not have to tell anyone what was going on, causing me to feel trapped in my sin. I was able to overcome entrapment once I learned why the enemy was doing this to me. He did this to insert fear on the inside of me, along with many other false thoughts. He would also do this in order to stop the flow of a pure anointing. If you do not conquer the enemy's scheme against you, it can cause you to move towards error. When one moves in error it positions them to be mislead in the spirit realm. One will be more likely to move out of their emotions or more open to be used by other sources outside of God.

As I look back now, I recognize why I encountered these situations, it was the call that was on my life. There are certain demons that are assigned to specific callings, we will walk through these in Chapter 6. It is essential for you to be able to identify yourself in the Spirit or having parents, and/or leaders to see the prophetic call upon your life. I honor and appreciate the God in my parents, because they were able to help guide and raise, myself and four other prophetic children, which can be challenging.

I have felt led to share my personal journey because some of you may have experienced or may be experiencing now what I have encountered. I want you to know that you aren't crazy or weird. You should not ignore the things you hear, see and sense because it is God speaking to you. Once you identify, you can walk in the fullness of who God has called you to be.

One of the ways that I was cultivated efficiently and precisely in my gifts was being active in an Apostolic Prophetic house. The teaching and training from my amazing Apostle Charissee had an affect on me at a very young age. For this reason, by the time I was thirteen years old, I preached my very first sermon. I became a prime demonstration that a child could be activated in their gifts and that age did not matter in the Spirit. In Chapter 7, I will describe more key characteristics of prophets. Although everyone is not called to the Office of the Prophet, everyone should desire to prophesy. How do you know if you are called to prophesy?

1 Corinthians 14:1

Follow after charity, and desire spiritual gifts, but rather that ye may prophesy.

God wants us to be accelerated in our spiritual gifts operating through love along with the desire to prophesy/ declaring His word. A lot of times churches or leaders may think a prophet only has the authority to prophesy. However, this is not true we all should covet to prophesy. If you yearn to do it and activate in faith, then God will respond by giving you the words to say. As a young boy, I always wanted to speak the Word of the Lord, but I was ignorant to the level of sacrifice the anointing required. Many times as young people or adults, we want things to happen on our time or want God to move without being faithful. In order to receive a pure anointing to excel in the prophetic or any call, it cost. Through training, mentorships and my own personal experience, I have learned it cost a sacrifice to sustain the anointing. We can obtain and maintain our gifts, but in order for the anointing to sustain us, God has shown me that we are going to be tried by fire. "In order to produce the fire, you have to go through the fire"- Prophetess Shauntae Warren. In other words, you are going to be tried by people and by life circumstances, but when you come out you will endure promise. So in doing so, there will be times where you will be in a season of refraining from others. This a time when God is telling you not to go out or to not say certain things. All of this, of course, is based on your willingness and surrenderance to the Lord. Trust me, this is not an easy or comfortable process. In this season, you, the vessel are in a time of stretching and development. You will need to remain in prayer, giving God your best sacrifice. God will see you are willing to surrender your will to hear His voice. For example, a sacrifice I give is sleeping on the floor which enables me to be spiritually in tune with the will of God. Your sacrifice will be a crushing, a dying to self-will and self desires essentially making you more humble and pliable for God to use.

A prophetic vessel must be in a solid Apostolic Prophetic house of worship. Under this type of house, it will ensure your gift is being stirred up by the proper leadership. Your leadership will be able to see and locate you in the Spirit, guiding you to become trained and equipped in the realm of the prophetic. Nowadays, we see a lot of people who are just activating themselves and going on social media and things of that nature, this is not of God. A lot of times we find that people always want the title and recognition, but don't want the responsibility or accountability with the call. However, we all must go through a process to get to purpose before we are put out on a platform. One may get a platform before time, and this happens a lot when the vessel is wanting to move in the prophetic or they know they are called which enables zeal (great energy or enthusiasm in pursuit of a cause or an objective). Zeal is not bad because it gives great motivation behind any objective. The problem is when zeal is misplaced it pushes us ahead of time, causing the vessel to miss the process in which God will equip them for ministry. For this very reason, you have to make sure you have the proper zeal guided by authorized leadership.

Once you answer the call there is going to be something that God requires of you, things He requires of all of us as yielded vessels. He will need us living a lifestyle of holiness and prayer. A lifestyle of holiness and prayer are important because when you start walking in the call then a lot of distractions and blockages will come to hinder progress. My assignment in this chapter is to get you to see that you have been called to prophesy the Word of the Lord no matter your background, current knowledge or past.

As mentioned before, a lot of times I would sleep on the floor or give up other things that made me comfortable. I wanted to show God how desperately I wanted the anointing and that I was willing to give up anything for Him. In the Bible, it tells us God honors sacrifice.

Hebrews 13:16

But to do good and to communicate forget not: for with such sacrifices God is well pleased

Psalm 54:6

I will sacrifice unto thee: I will praise thy name, O Lord; for it is good.

That's exactly what I did. Some of you may need to do the same as well, give up something you love daily to show God how badly you yearn for more of Him. God has picked and ordained you to speak His word. There will be some that read this book that are called to the Office of a Prophet or just to prophesy. Either way, God has need of you and wants you to begin to speak in the Earth. As I began to write this very book, God told me I am called for chapter one because a lot of young people in ministry don't even know they have gifts or how to move in them. There are nine spiritual gifts; Word of Knowledge, Word of Wisdom, Gift of Healing, Faith, Miracle, Prophecy, Diversity of Tongues, Interpretation of Tongues and Discernment.

Even those who are not are believers have giftings and a call on their life, they are just not fully aware of it. As a young adult today, I know what it has felt like to be ignorant of such information and because of that God has put it on my heart to share about the prophetic. Here's some background on me; Weshaun Warren. I grew up in church, I really had no option considering my parents were leaders and worked closely with the pastors. I would faithfully be at church from the time I got out of school until the next day. Sometimes I would even go into prayer meetings before school. I became accustomed to this lifestyle of being at church all the time. During this time I wasn't really being activated, I was enjoying my childhood with other friends and family. One day that all changed when Apostle Charisse gathered all the young people to the altar. We began to cry out and travail "Jesus" until we could no longer. I was only about seven years old at this time, with barely any understanding of what was going on. The good thing is, as a result of prayer and constantly being around Apostle who always had a revelation to teach, I was able to have a foundation of God and who I was in Him. She would call me "Prophet", speaking directly to who God had destined me to become. God used her to stir up the gifts on the inside of me early. It was at the age of 13 when I preached my first sermon and carried the responsibility of the youth on that Sunday. At that point I was entering into a realm I had no clue existed, later known as the prophetic. God used me in a way that people never have seen at my age, I was honored to be a used vessel. In that very moment, I promised God if he used me, I would follow Him the rest of my life.

Just like many other teenagers, as I grew older I ventured off the course God had for my life. I got involved in a lot of things I shouldn't have. However, in all my mess I always found myself in a place physically, emotionally or mentally where I did not fit in. I tried and tried to force myself to fit in or to do things to be accepted. At the same time, I was still being insulated. When I went to college, I still wasn't living the life God had called me to. It wasn't until I came home for a semester that God began to deal with me. I thank God for my parents who can hear in the Spirit because my mom just straight up told me "You out of alignment." From that conversation with her, I knew I had to get my life together. As I spent my time at home away from the party scene and no good friends, I was refreshed, renewed and reunited with fire and a pure anointing. My decision to come home for a semester has resulted in me walking in the office of the prophet today. Now God has called me to share knowledge and insight with other young prophets, youth who are called to be prophetic ministers or some who are called to the Office of the Prophet.

Chapter 2

THE MEANING OF THE PROPHETIC

In this chapter, you will learn further details about the prophetic realm giving you more comprehension and requirements of walking in this realm.

The prophetic realm is a realm that all may not flow in, but if you are reading this book I want you to know that there is a prophetic call on your life. You will start to be stirred up even as you continue to read further. One of the most important keys to know and remember is that God gives us the grace to walk in this type of anointing, not man. In the realm of the prophetic; miracles, signs, and wonders are produced and the Word of the Lord becomes clearer than usual. When you tap into the prophetic realm everything becomes accelerated, what might have taken three weeks can happen in three days. Or even what may have taken years can happen instantly, according to the faith of the vessel. The prophetic realm consists of different prophetic systems and functions such as; prophetic people, churches, and the office of the prophet. Prophetic churches are places of worship where the leader believes in the prophetic anointing.

1 Thessalonians 5:20

Despise not prophesyings

The leader teaches his or her sheep the functions and trains them to move in the realm of the prophetic. A prophetic person believes in the prophetic anointing. They are conscious of the functions of being a prophetic vessel and are open to receive and to give the Word of the Lord. The prophetic realm comes from one of the nine spiritual gifts called prophecy, categorized under the mouth gifts, the vocal gifts, or some may say gifts of utterance. In addition, the gift of diversity of tongues and interpretation of tongues are under this category as well. Prophecy is a gift where one can speak directly what God is saying by being revealed the heart of God. Prophets are not the only ones who can prophesy, we all can.

Acts 2:18

And on my servants and on my handmaidens I will pour out in those days of my Spirit, and they shall prophesy:

1 Corinthians 14:39

Wherefore, brethren, covet to prophesy, and forbid not to speak with tongues.

These scriptures state that we all have the ability and should desire to prophesy. God is no respecter of persons (**Acts 10:34**), that is to say, you can prophesy no matter your background, skin color, gender, or shortcomings.

Another gift, under the gifts of utterance, is the gift of speaking in the diversity of tongues.

1 Corinthians 12:10

To another working of miracles; to another prophecy; to another discerning of spirits; to another divers kinds of tongues; to another the interpretation of tongues:

While the gift of tongues is activated and the anointing is high your tongues can continue to change while you are praying by the way of the Spirit. This is a gift that has been activated in my life, so a lot of times when I am in prayer the power of God comes into my atmosphere then my tongues will change. This is something you can receive all you have to do is receive it, and walk in it, and it's yours. This gift is important to the prophetic realm, because it is an unknown tongue that cannot be understood by the enemy; which means, God can commune with you Spirit to Spirit giving you the words to say.

Finally, in the vocal gifts, there is the gift of interpretation of tongues. According to **1 Corinthians 12:10,** we know that by the way of the Spirit one can interpret what is being spoken in the unknown language. Remember this is Spirit to Spirit, tongues cannot be known with our natural understanding because it's only a Heavenly language that our Spirit man and God understands. The gift of speaking in tongues and interpretation are used to perfect the gift of prophecy and even the revelation gifts (Word of Wisdom, Word of Knowledge and Discerning of Spirits). This can be seen when God gives you a word of wisdom or a strategic plan to give to someone else to guide them and steer them in the right path. Also, God can release a word of knowledge where He can show you something about one's past which helps gain the attention of the recipient. He may make known a past wound in order to heal and to get them excited about what He is about to do in their life. Lastly, another gift used to perfect the prophetic is the gift of discernment. When operating in this gift God will show you or give you a sense of a situation or the atmosphere. He does this to give us insight on how to move forward accordingly. God is trying to get us to see that there is another level of anointing that He wants to give us. When we are yielded to Him, He will give us these gifts to use us as a concrete expression of His glory in the earth realm. We will be able to live our lives with supernatural power but in the natural realm. Some other things to know in the prophetic realm are basic terms, we will learn even more prophetic terms as well in part two of this book.

The term **Naba** means to bubble up or be stirred up. One can be stirred up when God releases His power or a word in your belly. It begins to stir up the more, especially if it cannot be released at the moment. As prophets, we don't conjure up things or read people, but it is through the stirring of the Holy Spirit that we speak the oracles of God. At the appointed time God will charge you to release the prophetic word, this is known as Nataf. *Nataf* means to drop like rain. Usually when the word is spoken, it will come out with a fiery anointing behind it. This occurs as a result of the vessel being stirred up in the presence of God and for those who walk in the office of the prophet. Prophets spend time in the secret place and God will begin to invade their atmospheres by giving them Rhema Words at any given time. Now something to note there is a difference from the Spirit of Prophecy, Gift of Prophecy and walking in the Office of the Prophet. If the Spirit of Prophecy is present anyone that is in that atmosphere may start to hear and or see or sense in the Spirit. They will begin to feel the unction to prophesy due to the Spirit of God being heavy in the atmosphere. (The Gift of Prophecy and the Office of the Prophet will be elaborated on in further chapters.) Another basic term is **Chabod**; the weight of God's glory. The vessel has no choice but to yield to the authority of Jesus Christ when the Chabod glory is present. Those who are even around, we be able to feel God's thick presence making it hard to stand or move. We must be consistent in our prayer lives that way we can handle the weight of His glory. This is an amazing thing to experience because in this atmosphere God can move in a mighty way. We are able to see the miraculous take place in the earth realm. Just as any subject we must be knowledgeable in order to function efficiently and effectively. Any prophetic vessel in the correct house and submitted under the appropriate leadership will be able to attain teaching and be cultivated fully. As you continue reading, you will gain more knowledge of the power of the prophetic.

Chapter 3

POWER & THE PROPHETIC

Prayer

It is pivotal that we remain in prayer as prophetic vessels, especially when it comes to being a carrier of God's glory. As we learned in the earlier chapters, we should spend more time in prayer than we do prophesying. When we go deeper in prayer it unlocks the secrets of Heaven, God reveals His secret things to His servants the prophets.

Mark 11:24

Therefore I tell you, whatever you ask for in prayer, believe that you have received it, and it will be yours.

To put it differently, whatever we ask when we pray, it shall be given unto us. Have you ever received a Word of Knowledge, accurate, down to the nail? Prophetic ministers are able to gain that information from the Heavens because they have spent time in the secret place. Prayer and the prophetic go hand and hand, you shouldn't have one without the other. This is a keynote to put down because this gives you access to the heavens. Prayer is so powerful it allows you an advance on the move of God. When you are in prayer God can reveal things to come, solutions, circumstances, and the heart of man, even while praying in the Spirit. When you are praying in the Spirit, your spirit is now in tune with God's heart allowing you to have insight on what He is feeling or saying. Some people may speak in tongues during a prophecy or before, be aware that this happens because their spirit man and God are in communication. This, of course, is an unknown tongue that the enemy doesn't understand, but it is Spirit to Spirit with God. Prophetic ministers may not even hear anything at the moment concerning the person or situation. We must not allow fear or doubt to creep in for this is an opportunity for us to prophetically pray. Prophetic prayer is speaking the Word of the Lord by decreeing and declaring. There are many times when people are in this situation and instead of prophetically praying they sadly lie on God by conjuring up words to say or fail to even go up to the person God has told them to prophesy over. When in reality, we can go speak life, decreeing and declaring the Word over them. As the giver of the Word, we have to use faith when we declare God's Word, that way the receiver will accept and believe. In doing this, it is a form of exhortation, speaking to an audience and praying prophetically. As you are growing, it is key to remember considering you will find times in the prophetic where you need to pray. It is through prayer that you may begin to hear clearly what God is saying. Keep in mind that any prophetic minister or prophet must be an intercessor, but an intercessor may not be a prophet.

An Intercessor is one who is called to the ministry of prayer. After reading *Building a Strong Prayer Wall* by Dr. Charissee.There are five different types of intercessors:

General- One who can pray fervently and effectively for any topic, with or without open request or vision.

30

Crisis- Operates best in times of trauma, drama, and crisis. Which enables them to pray with a direct assignment from God.

Warfare- Has the authority by God to go into the realm of darkness, confront the forces of Satan and his demons.

Personal- Whose assignment is to pray for the man and women of God, who are activated in the five-fold ministry.

Specialist- Can pray on a specific topic and or area of a situation.

Which one are you?

Prayer is so powerful and useful when it comes to the prophetic due to the power, strength, and accuracy that follows behind the prophetic word given. Prayer is direct communication from you and God. Did you know that there are certain ways we can approach God? I am not suggesting that your way of praying is incorrect. Rather, I am going to give another perspective to help in times of prayer. The first step is adoration, this is giving God praise and worship, all while acknowledging who He is. For instance, saying; " We honor you Lord", "There is no one like you", "We approach your throne of grace humbly." When this is done, it's what I like to call knocking on the door of Heaven. We are showing and telling God how much we appreciate Him and how it is all about Him, not about us.

The next step is Confession. Confession is recognizing that we all fall short of the Glory of God every day and we must confess our sins, asking God for forgiveness. When we confess what we are feeling or going through according to our situation, or our sins, we enter into a place of freedom and healing. Our heart is now free because we are willing, telling our Father what is on our mind and heart. I always propose the question; would you rather someone be forced to tell you that they love you, or genuinely tell you themselves? I used this as an example because God loves when we come willingly and genuinely to Him. Not when we are forced so it means something to Him and it pulls on His heart. When this is done then He begins to pour out unto us, giving us our freedom and or blessings. You are being responsible for your actions, which is pleasing unto God. A lot of times my dad would know that I had done something wrong, but just wanted me to own up to it. Eventually, when I did tell him it enabled him to trust me more, love me more, and give more accountability according to what I can handle.

Next, we should have a grateful heart and be thankful.

1 Chronicles 16:34

Give thanks unto the Lord

We need to thank Him for who He is. A lot of times people thank Him for what He has done, not for who He is. This is a time in prayer where we open our mouths and hearts to the King of Kings. Now don't get me wrong, we should still thank Him for what He has done, what He is doing, and what He is going to do. In all, we just can't forget the fact He died on the cross that we may live life, and live it more abundantly. The last structure to prayer is supplication, which is making your request known.

Philippians 4:6
Be careful for nothing; but in everything by prayer and supplication with thanksgiving let your request be made known to God.

Philippians 4:6 explains that we can ask anything in His name. In this time of prayer, you can pray for others, and yourself asking for your heart's desires. Still ending with giving Him thanks and honor and glory. All and all prayer is critical because it is how we see the Kingdom of God in our lives. In the Bible, there were many that had strong prayer lives and prayed for specific things.

These include:

• Hannah prayed a prayer of praise and adoration to God

• Jonah prayed a prayer of salvation

• David prayed a prayer of deliverance

• The prayer of Jabez where he cried out to God

• The Lord's prayer

These are some of the secret tips to activating God's power. Although, we talked about a few we did not cover all. Note that sacrificing and fasting are powerful weapons. These two things are also key components in releasing the power of God. Sacrificing is giving up something that feeds the flesh, but instead, we are feeding our spirit man. Think of the natural man, just as you eat, you begin to get bigger and grow. It's like it unto the Spirit man the more you feed and nurture; the greater and faster it develops. The difference in the Spirit and in the natural is that the Spirit can handle the weight and only gets bigger in a good way. So when God sees this He honors it because it's a sacrifice if our hearts are postured rightly. Then God will respond filling us with His power, which is the greatest thing one can experience. Young people misunderstand the power of sacrifice and fasting. We want things so quickly and on our time, which is a dangerous place to be in. In that type of mindset or posture, we can miss the move of God in our lives, or hold the process longer. All in all, we have to understand that as we begin to ascend (go up) in Him with these tips given, the power of God will start to descend (bring down) on the earth. As we lift up our prayer and sacrifices unto the Lord, then He will respond with sending His glory down to us on earth. A few things to note is that power is important when it comes to the prophetic, it enables accuracy to deliver the prophetic message. Here is a list of three different types of power that is important when it comes to the prophetic.

Exousia- the power of authority, one that has been given influence.

Dunamis- Gods Dynamic power, gives strength, force, might, capability.

Kratos- mighty power.

When you go forth in prayer you will gain power, which will enable you to move forward in the supernatural. This only happens when one is submitted to God through prayer.

Faith & Praise

One piece of advice that God tells us in the book of **Matthew 16:19**, is that He has given us access to the kingdom. The creative power and tip to prophecy is faith. The prophetic ministry stands on faith, as we know faith is the substance of things hoped for and the evidence of things not seen (**Hebrews 11:1**). We need to know that faith is not a natural thing, but it is a supernatural substance. "When faith becomes mature then it is raw" as Apostle Charissee says frequently. During my study on faith, I came to a concrete understanding that faith becomes open and responsive. In other words, you can believe but it takes action with faith that causes God to respond. When you have the Gift of Faith, it destroys all fear and hindrances. Strong bulldog faith reaches God and allows Him to give us access and authority to enter into new dimensions of God's glory. Faith joins the power to the prophetic, causing the believer to actually pursue their word. When we proclaim, declare, and testify what God has promised. In return, it creates the promise into an tangible substance. **Romans 12:3** tells us that it is according to one's faith that can determine the timing of the prophecy. Faith is the secret agent that produces the manifestation of our prophetic words. This means that we have to trust God, rather we understand or not. The Bible declares faith without works is dead (**James 2:26**), so we have to prove our faith through our actions. This can be displayed through praise, word choice, or simply how you live. For example, let's say you live in a house and want to move but do not have the requirements to move. Faith says even if the money isn't there "I'm going to go look for my new home." Even cleaning and taking care of the home I have currently. The Bible tells us we have to be good stewards over what He has given us. Faith and praise are keys to accelerating the move of God. Using faith and praise together will cause an advance in the Spirit realm, also will show the recipient of the Word to have hope until it comes into existence. When we use both components we are acting by faith and believing what He says, therefore, the hand of God moves instantly.

God's Glory

God's glory in the prophetic is a sight to see young people. I love seeing and experiencing the power of God come over me. There is no controlling it, and it is not a scary feeling at all either. Instead, it feels great like powerful energy being released, making me feel like I could do anything. It is something as Christians we don't want to miss out on. When the glory is present miraculous things can take place, like healing, favor, and freedom from oppressive and depressive spirits. The weight of God's glory (**Chabod**) brings power, authority and wealth. When the **Chabod** glory comes down it also arrest every demonic spirit in the atmosphere. So even if any spirit on the inside of you is trying to keep you bound, then it no longer can. This is due to the Dunhams power that is in the atmosphere. When the glory realm and the prophetic come together into one atmosphere, it creates a supernatural power. This power cannot be stopped by the enemy, yourself or anyone operating in the soulish realm. Once again, this type of environment will evoke healing, deliverance, and miracles to take place. When the glory comes in, the vessel must yield their authority to our Lord & Saviour Jesus Christ, giving honor to the Spirit of Christ by moving out of the way. Many preachers today are so concerned about this wonderful revelation they have gotten by God as they were preparing for what to say to the congregation. They want to read all their notes and tell every detail of the revelation so others can be moved. In retrospect, it's not us but it's God moving through us. For this reason, when the power of God is present and He wants to have His way, we cannot try to contain or control it. If you try to control or contain the move of God, it can cause someone to miss their breakthrough, deliverance, healing, prophetic word and etc. I have experienced numerous times when I minister the Lord will begin to move. Any humble prophet when this occurs needs to yield their authority to God. It is at this time when I choose to flow with the Spirit and healing usually takes place, and or I flow through the prophetic vein and speak the Word of the Lord.

If you desire to walk in this level of anointing, you should walk in all Fruits of the Spirit because of the reason that our gifts flow through our heart. God, He wants a humble vessel that will flow with His heart. In order to have His heart, you have to be submitted to the Fruits of the Spirit. Many leaders today have gifts, but neglect having the heart of God. Meaning that they are not moving in God's divine principles. The Bible talks to us about walking in love, humility and more. The Glory of God is something that we should never take for granted. If we want to see more miracles, signs, and wonders in the earth, there needs to be more pure vessels yielded and ready. God has placed this book on my heart so that we as prophetic vessels can walk in a pure and humble anointing. We are going to began to see more miracles in the earth than usual, but God wants to use pure and humble vessels that He can trust with the weight of His glory.

Chapter 4

WHAT HINDERS THE PROPHETIC GIFT

There are many spirits and actions that can hinder your prophetic flow. In this day and time, we are surrounded by a lot of different distractions and hindrances in the atmosphere. The Bible tells us in **John 15:14**, we are in this world but we are not of this world. There will be a lot of times, where we become faced with temptations that can taint the purity of our gift. Through this chapter, we will discuss some spirits that can hinder your flow in the prophetic realm. It's good for us to be aware, that way you can identify if there's something that you need to be freed from.

Pride

The spirit of pride is something that God despises amongst all other spirits, this one tells God, He is not in control. I wanted to deal with pride first because this spirit is a sabotage spirit that will bring anyone down.

Proverbs 16:18-19

Pride goes before destruction and haughtiness before a fall. Better to live humbly with the poor than to share plunder with the proud.

This scripture shows that when operating in pride it will cause you to be blinded by the move of God, and you will start walking in self righteousness. Self righteousness leads to a spirit of error. This spirit loves to have control over the people of God. It will use people for their money, gifts, and talents. According to the Word, pride will be exposed and brought down. For this reason, pride is one of the main spirits used to attack the prophetic voices of God. It works in deceitful ways to have us get caught up in ourselves and what we think and feel should be done, which is moving in the spirit of error. If you notice you may be dealing with the spirit of pride, it is important that you go through deliverance so you can be set free. According to **James 4:6**, He will grace the humble and also exalt the humble. We should walk in humility because I have been told and shown, "The lower you go, the higher God will take you."

Sin

Sin is any action, deed, or thought that is contrary to the Word of God (**1 John 3:4**). All sin overall is a hindrance to our walk with God and the realm of the prophetic. In fact, it has the power to cause a spiritual clog, where you feel stuck and can't let go of the bad pollution or negative things on the inside of you. Also, in this state, it is difficult to receive more from God. Sin will cause a barrier between you and God in the prophetic realm. If this takes place, the prophet usually will shy away from his/her prophetic call and the enemy will begin rejoicing. Ultimately, that happens because he or she either is no longer hearing accurately from God and or the conviction is not as strong. Under these circumstances, this can cause the vessel to be stagnated in their walk with God. Prophetic vessels must cover themselves in prayer because the devil wants to make a mockery out of us.

When walking in sin you will have a hard time entering into the throne room, and even in an atmosphere of sin. To give an example, there have been times where I was speaking and God showed me there was sin in the camp. Before I went forth to speak, we had to worship more and I had to lay hands on the people to cast out every perverse spirit that was in operation trying to stop the flow of God. Any vessel who walks in sin is not pure, and may not function under the anointing. The Bible declares gifts and callings come without repentance, but the anointing cost (**Romans 11:29**). It is under the anointing we see the miraculous transpire, so if the vessel is in sin then healing, or deliverance can't happen. In order to walk in healing, you have to be pure, in order to walk in deliverance, you have to be clean. Otherwise, you can transfer what you are going through onto the people of God, and the blood will be on your hands. We all sin and fall short of the glory of God but we need to repent and move forward.

Negative Words

A prophetic vessel must stay away from negative atmospheres, where words are being spoken over the vessel's life. Negative seeds can be planted on the inside of you concerning your gift, your self-esteem, and future. Negativity can come in forms of unbelief, doubt, gossip, slander, or being judgmental/critical. The Lord has made prophetic vessels sensitive for the reason of being sensitive to the spiritual realm. Therefore, hearing negativity all the time will create false seeds inside the vessel's spirit and can encourage the vessel to stop speaking or believing God. Or even worse, they can enter into warfare that will cause his/her gift to be tainted. Likewise, we must watch what we put in our ear gates or eye gates because negativity is easier to gravitate towards than positivity.

Proverbs 18:21

Life and death are in the power of the tongue.

As Prophets, we can't speak blessings and curses out of the same mouth. I can't walk around speaking and listening to negativity all the time. I have to think, act and speak like Christ. Over time, I have learned to watch the music I allow in my spirit because without knowing, it was causing a slow flow of the anointing in my life. The moment I replaced secular music with worship music was the moment I noticed I was hearing the Lord clearer. It is our responsibility to be sensitive and open to the Spirit of God meaning we need to guard our prophetic system. As well as, watch who we allow to speak into our lives and impart into us because it is possible for spirits to transfer. Impartation goes a long way, you may not be aware of it at the moment but later on, there will be results of who groomed you; poorly or greatly. Surrounding yourself with positive people and positive words will push your faith in God. On the other hand, negativity has the ability to discourage your connection from you and God.

Fear

Fear is another huge factor that will cause a hindrance to the flow of the prophetic realm. Fear is one of the roots of Satan's camp. This spirit will try to have you intimidated of the call or someone else in authority. It has an objective goal to close the prophet's mouth. Fear will have you operating in lies, knowingly or unknowingly. One will lie just to cover themselves, or even lie because they are scared of the outcome of the situation. You cannot operate out of fear in the prophetic. Why? Prophecy is activated and moves upon faith, fear is the exact opposite.

Therefore, if I have a fear that I won't hear God in clarity, it can cause me to lie to people as I am prophesying, especially when giving a prophetic word to those in authority. You have to master walking by faith and being completely obedient no matter the circumstance or outcome. Fear will have you moving with the wave of man, instead of the wave of glory. What I mean by that is, one who walks in fear is afraid of what people will think or say about them. This type of fear will propel one to lie or make decisions that are going to uplift themselves or have people accept them. Do not fall into the temptation of wanting to be accepted by man, rather ride the wave of glory because as prophets sometimes everyone isn't going to like you, or what you have to say. In all, the spirit of fear comes also to bring hurt and pain to you. I have personally dealt with this as a young prophet, I was always afraid of not being accepted or accurate. I would tend to look at people's faces and reactions when I was speaking to them, or would just hear how some people bashed the ministry of the prophets. I retain hearing people and leaders criticize those who were young, like me, going forth in ministry. Praise be to God I was under the right leadership because of all the knowledge and understanding I was taught. I learned when prophesying you can't be moved by faces or body posture. You have to depend and trust in God no matter what, this is faith in activation. Sometimes as prophets we can even see faces and the person is receptive, then we feel like we should keep digging because we see we are on point, we cannot do that either. In later chapters, we will begin to understand how one can move into familiar spirits and even divination. To sum up, fear will hinder your prophetic gift but faith will stir you up and propel you to move further in destiny. Break off the fear!

Disobedience

Next, disobedience is another matter that can block the prophetic from being stirred to its full capacity. When we fail to obey what God tells us, it puts a hold on the prophecies we give. As one disobeys God, the power in what he/she speaks becomes low. Which can really take an individual, off course, this can also stop the move of God in our own lives. This spirit can cause you to not hear the voice of God clearly as well.

Romans 5:14

For as by one man's disobedience many were made sinners. So by the obedience of one shall be made righteous.

That is to say, if you choose to disobey God then you can cause someone else's life to be messed up. This is significant to the prophetic vessel to grasp, that way when God tells you to speak, you will only say what He says; nothing more, nothing less. There may be times where you may hear God speaking concerning an individual but you cannot release the word unless God tells you and or it's judged by your spiritual covering. Many prophets today, especially the ones that are just coming around have no home training, sometimes prophetic vessels release whatever they hear whenever and however. The Word of God states to everything there is a time and a season, so you don't wanna release a prophetic word out of season. I can't express enough, that training and being under the right prophetic leader is pivotal to your growth. Disobedience will prohibit the move of God, my dad said it best "Delayed obedience is still disobedience". With this in mind, continue to be obedient to the voice of God.

Wrong Character

As Prophets, God watches our character. Our character must remain integrable and humble in the eyes of God. It doesn't matter if you have been hearing God clearly, if your character is not right then you are not a true Prophet. The right character consists of being loving, humble, honest, integrable and using discretion. There will be times God shows you something about someone or they may tell you themselves, it is your job to keep all things confidential. We are seeing in today's prophets most can prophesy accurately, but their left-hand ministry is jacked up. When I say left-hand ministry, I mean that behind the scene there are some areas that have to be dealt with. That particular vessel may operate out of hurt, rejection, and or perverse spirits, which makes the vessel impure. Through teaching under my Apostle, I learned that our gifts flow from our hearts and whatever is in our hearts while we are ministering will come out or become visible at some point and time. I continuously ask God to fix my character, that I will not make a mockery or shame out of His anointing. We should want to have the mantle of humility, not the spirit of humility but the mantle. The difference is that when the mantle is on you then it rests upon you. When you have the spirit of humility it can be lifted at any given time. As a prophet, I pray for the mantle, to keep me under submission to God's will and keep God in control. Integrity is an important characteristic to attain as well. Presently, we see prophets put people on blast, or embezzle money from the congregation. I am exposing these types of behavior to sharpen your discernment and make you aware. If someone is operating in this manner, it does not mean they don't have a prophetic gift. What it does mean or show is that they haven't dealt with everything that has been in their hearts. Remember this, gifts and callings come without repentance, but the anointing cost! (**Romans 11:29**). There is an important lesson to be learned; we can operate in our gifts from God all we want. However, if what we are doing behind the scenes doesn't match what we preach or teach, we are not in God's divine will. He calls us to be like Him, living pure and holy lifestyles.

Lack of Faith

The foundation of prophecy is built on faith. Hence, why a lack of faith can be detrimental to any prophetic vessel. If the vessel does not have faith when speaking God's word, it can either delay or the word doesn't come into manifestation. In order to move into this realm, there has to be a level of faith that is released. Upon faith being released, God can see that you know He can do the impossible. Our faith must increase so that we can prophesy.

Romans 12:6

Having then gifts differing according to the grace that is given to us, whether prophecy, let us prophesy according to the proportion of faith.

Which is to say, in order to speak a new car into someone's life, you have to know that God is able to do it first. Faith accelerates the move of God and is a key to the supernatural, meaning faith allows us to expect and receive the unseen things. In the school of the prophetic training, we learn there is a difference between the Gift of Faith and the Spirit of Faith. When there is a Gift of Faith, you have unlocked one of the attributes of the Holy Spirit, meaning strong faith dwells in you. In the Spirit of Faith, you may believe God but it can be determined by the situation or how things are looking. Faith is a key to the supernatural, if you believe God can do it then He will respond. Nevertheless, there is a distinction between believing God vs believing in God. Believing in God means you know that He exists and acknowledge His presence. On the other hand, one who believes God they know and understand that He can do the impossible and they give Him full control. At the end of the day, you need both to believe Him and believe in Him.

Example of Faith when prophesying:

Someone has $500 in their bank account but God gives a word to you concerning their new home. Let's say you take their current status into consideration and begin to question God by asking Him, "Now how is that going to happen?" At this moment, your faith is freezing the keys from being released. Rather, you should have faith that God can do exactly what He says despite of what you see in the natural.

Lack of Prayer

A lack of prayer has the ability to stop the prophetic flow, specifically young prophets. Why? We as young people can be easily moved by the things of this world. You must protect your prophetic gift by staying in prayer.

Psalm 91:1

He that dwelleth in the secret place of the Most High shall abide under the shadow of the Almighty.

As young people, we will encounter a lot of trials and tribulations in this world. Therefore, it is imperative that we stay in the secret place. The secret place is where God can download revelatory knowledge on the inside of you. Not only that, but this will keep you in a position of humility. That is key as young people to know in destiny that we need to have hearts of flesh (**Ezekiel 36:26**). God is going to use us, we are the next generation. Nowadays, people tend to get big heads as soon as God uses them. Hence why it is essential we stay humble that way The Lord can continue to use us in greater measures.

1 Peter 5:6

Humble yourselves therefore under the mighty hand of God, that he may exalt you in due time;

Prayer is vital to unlocking the supernatural, this is what goes before the throne room of grace. When we pray and our hearts are in right standing, God will hear you and your request will be answered in His time. Prayer in the prophetic realm is what keeps us pure and humble. The ability to sacrifice to God indicates to Him that we don't care about what we are doing at the moment or how we may feel. We must be willing to give up our schedules and overcome personal feelings to pray without ceasing. My big sister Brianna Warren said, "God honors unorthodox prayer." It's at those random times of prayer and adoration to the King that He cherishes. The more time spent with Him, the more trust is given and He can begin to reveal more of His secrets. As a prophet, we should spend more time in our prayer closet then we do prophesying. Above all, I challenge you to answer the mandate of prayer.

Part Two

THE MINISTRY OF THE PROPHET

Chapter 5

BRINGING THE GIFT FORTH

As you are reading this chapter, you will begin to feel a prophetic word on the inside of you. You will learn how to use your gift, methods of prophecy, and hearing the voice of God.

There are a few methods to prophecy:

The Gift of Prophecy:

The Gift of Prophecy is a resident anointing in the vessel, where he or she can prophesy once stirred or activated. This often times happens when a seasoned Apostle or Prophet oversees the prophetic exercise. Training and activation develops the prophetic gift on the inside of the vessel. It gives strength and stretches the vessel, preparing them for prophetic ministry.

The Spirit of Prophecy:

When the Spirit of Prophecy is released then anyone can prophesy under the Spirit of God and a mantle is dropped. As a result, those who may not even acknowledge God may hear or discern something in their spirit. This is because the anointing is high and the **Chabod** (weight of His glory) is present. In this type of atmosphere, no one can hardly move and everything yields to the presence of God. Let's say you bring a friend to church for the first time and during the service, the Spirit of Prophecy is released. After the service they tell you, "Man, that service was different. I felt something inside of me and I kept hearing the word joy." Ultimately, this was able to happen because the vessel was in an atmosphere conducive for the prophetic realm to flow.

Prophetic Preaching:

There is a Rhema Word. A word that is a right now word, for a right now people. Sometimes God will use the vessel to flow in this prophetic anointing, and speak over the people and prophesy. He or she may not teach, but will speak directly to what's going on in the atmosphere. When this happens the vessel has yielded their authority to the presence of God. It doesn't mean they're off or not speaking biblical principles, because a Rhema Word should still line up with the Word of God. God uses me a lot in this area where He shows me things or tells me what the people of God are in need of.

Prophetic Prayer:

Prophetic prayer is communicating the mind of God by foretelling an inspired Word of the Lord through a form of prayer. This also can be used often while prophesying as you speak over one's life.

Prophetic Song:

The Song of the Lord; singing out what God is saying. There are different types of songs one can sing during worship. Apostle Charissee goes into further detail about the worship experience in her book *Liquid Fire: School of the Prophetic Basic.*

Colossians 3:16

Let the word of Christ dwell in you richly in all wisdom; teaching and admonishing one another in psalms and hymns and spiritual songs, singing with grace in your hearts to the Lord.

The Song of the Lord- which is directed to the body of christ, by our father.

The Song of the Bridegroom- Jesus Christ sings a love song to the church.

Song of the Bride- we the church responds, with a love song back to God.

Songs of Deliverance- a word of knowledge is released to set souls free.

Song of Warfare- commanding demons to come subject to the power of God.

Prophetic Demonstration:

One who demonstrates God's power in the Earth realm. A vessel under the anointing, God will use them to lay hands. By doing so, souls can be set free, healed, and delivered. Also, this is where we have what we call the foot soldiers (dancers) that will wave banners and dance in the Spirit. The foot soldiers motions will be led by way of the Holy Ghost.

You must understand that there are various veins to flow in, concerning the prophetic realm. It goes beyond just prophesying verbally, but consist of dance, worship, praying and demonstration, as well.

Now it is pivotal that we follow the Spirit of God at all times. There may be moments where you won't hear anything when this occurs, you are being tested and you must not say anything. Sometimes, God will do that to see if the vessel is going to be obedient. We must be disciplined enough to say what God would have us to say, nothing more or less. When you don't hear anything, you must prophetically pray for the individual. Sometimes according to our faith, God will then release a word. Other times, God will give you a word, but it is not the time for you to release it. Remember, we learned that God reveals the secret things to His servants the prophets (Amos 3:7). So when this is done, it is our assignment to pray about what He has shown us for the individual.

As a young prophet, I had to stretch my faith. There have been times where I felt as if I wasn't old enough, or even worthy enough to prophesy. Aside from how you may feel, God has a called you to a purpose and you must answer the call on your life. Your life depends on it! This is something we must comprehend, as young prophets or even prophetic vessels. When God calls you to do assignments, you have to do them. I have learned this throughout my journey. Walking in this area of ministry, you have to know you are called without a shadow of a doubt. You need boldness, faith, prayer, and of course, love. I would strongly advise you to seek training from your Apostolic leader or someone qualified in the office of the Prophetic realm. This is strongly recommended with the purpose that you can be equipped and trained, just like any other gift we have.

Example: If one is good at basketball, yet they still have trainers, coaches and still go to practices to maintain their skill of basketball. There are Prophets with improper training, or no training at all; and this can cause them to be out of the vein of the prophetic. Essentially, not walking in humility and not being seasoned for the call God has placed on their life can hinder the way they minister the gift.

Although, I walk in the office of the Prophet, I am still under my Apostolic leadership and Pastors oversight. As a part of bringing forth your gift you will undergo a multitude of tests. God allows you to be drawn into uncomfortable situations or places to get you out of your comfort zone to see how you will respond in the midst. You will have to walk in boldness and love to deliver whatever God is saying.

Hearing the Voice

As we know there are two Kingdoms; the kingdom of darkness and the Kingdom of light. While studying God showed me there is another realm. There is the devil's kingdom, where we see an "evil". Then there's the kingdom of this world, which we call the "earth realm."Lastly, the Kingdom of light known as the "heaven." With that being said, there are three voices that anyone can hear; the devil's voice, your own voice and the voice of God.

The Devil's Voice

The devil's voice is anything that goes against what God is saying. The enemy will repeat whatever he wants you to do, in order to bring confusion, fear, and doubt. The main point when identifying the devil's voice is that he will say anything that goes against the laws and principles of God. He will try to compete with God. For the most part, trying to bring confusion in your mind, especially by constantly repeating what he is trying to get you to accomplish. It is important that when you hear this voice, that you identify it and rebuke it in Jesus name.

James 4:7,

If we resist the devil he shall flee.

Your Own Voice

Your own voice talks a lot from the soulish realm (mind, imagination, memory, and emotions). This voice is sent to bring fear on the inside of you, causing you to second guess what God is telling you to do. It doesn't all the time go against what He is saying, but it will have you think twice about it. Example: You are walking in the store and you hear God say "Go to that person and just give them a hug." You instantly start to second guess with thoughts like "I don't know if I should do that, that's a bit weird." When you do this, it causes confusion in the mind. Following your own voice can cause you to miss the timing of God, as well. Let's say in that situation you waited until you wanted to do it, now you can be set up for failure. Remember your voice will do whatever it can to enlighten itself. Encouraging you to do things when you feel like it, or doing things that will, in the end, cover you and also push you. See, we have to be very careful of this spirit because this leaves room for pride, and also the spirit of fear, two spirits that will hinder your prophetic gift.

For instance: God says "Go give those people a word." Now your own voice moves on its own timing, "Um when should I go? They look older, they might not receive." This then may allow the spirit of fear to set in and ultimately shut the mouth of the prophet.

God's Voice

God's voice is a clear and still, small voice (**1 Kings 19:12**). Now, God has made us all special and unique and because of that, we all hear Him in different ways. God uses nature, animals, and objects to speak to us at times, it is our flesh or self emotion that causes us to be confused. When I say different I mean, to some He may speak with an audible voice, to others through the Word of God, and to others dreams and visions. These are different ways that God speaks to us here on the earth. We have this misconception that God, Himself is gonna come down and speak to us like how we speak to one another. Now for some of us, we may hear Him so clear it feels as if He is present. In order to hear Him to that depth, you have to spend time with Him. When you wanna get to know someone you spend time with them, to build intimacy, causing you to know them and how they think even when they're not physically present. It is the same way with God, as prophetic vessels, we should spend more time on our face in the presence of God then we do prophesying. Plenty of times that's where prophets in today's world have gotten confused. When you spend time with Abba Father, as a by product, you become sensitive to the Spirit of God. So then some things He doesn't have to say directly, but because we know His heart then we gain a clear understanding. We must move when He speaks without any question, fear or doubt. Now God does give us grace and He may give you another opportunity to see these same people or to speak the word again. The main point is not moving until you hear. After you identify His voice, it's simple from here. Now you can move forward in the gift while living the lifestyle of holiness, that way your anointing can be pure. Then it will be about being obedient and speaking only when He says and what He says. Moving forward in the gift with faith, boldness, and love. All these things will grace you to prophesy deeply and precisely.

Spirit-Man

Did you know we all have a Spirit-man on the inside of us? I have learned a powerful tool, there is a distinction from hearing directly from God and hearing from your spirit man.

Your Spirit-man is the Holy Spirit living on the inside of you. Our human flesh covers our Spirit-man, the Bible tells us we are spirit, soul, and body (**1 Thessalonians 5:23**). In **Ephesians 4:23** reveals only the Spirit-man can renew our thoughts. God has shown me that when hearing from your spirit man it's more of a feeling than a direct answer from God. Although your Spirit should be led by God it is not a direct Rehma (right now word) from Him.

Example: You could be going to a party and your parents say I'm not feeling it, that's their Spirit-man speaking because it is not at peace with the situation. But then let's say you still go, now that doesn't mean something will happen, you actually can come back fine without anything happening. On the other hand, if they would have said God said, "Don't go." then there's a complete difference, why? Because it's more direct and speaks specifically to the situation causing a check in yourself and your spirit man, also to the flesh. Despite the fact that its two different ways, it's one in the same. My father, Pastor Wes Warren gives a perfect example of this, he says "Just like I am your dad, I am also your coach, and pastor. Although, I have different titles or at times could be speaking from different perspectives it's all still coming from the same person, Wes Warren."

Now let's see what God is saying:

Activation

This is a small activation to get your mind clear.

First, I would like you to gain a quiet atmosphere and close your eyes.

Next, ask God to show you something, it can be anything but one word only.

Now after you see or hear; write it down.

I saw money when I closed my eyes.

Now, simply I want you to close your eyes again and ask God "What are you saying concerning what you showed or told me."

Lastly, write it down.

I heard God saying, "I am releasing new money to you in this hour. But it is according to your obedience and sacrifice, you will receive." It is that simple. A lot of times we overthink hearing God's voice, which causes us to be confused. When really it is simple, the bible tells us in "Jeremiah 29:11". As well as, "Matthew 7:7", all we have to do is ask and he will speak to us.

Jeremiah 29:11

For I know the thoughts that I think toward you, saith the Lord, thoughts of peace, and not of evil, to give you an expected end.

Matthew 7:7

Ask, and it shall be given you; seek, and ye shall find; knock, and it shall be opened unto you:

Chapter 6

UNDERSTANDING SPIRITUAL WARFARE AND THE PROPHET

Living in today's society there are so many tactics that the enemy will try to use as a distraction to us as prophets and young people overall. As a young prophet growing up inside of the church, you would think that I was exempt from warfare. Well actually, that's who the enemy is after, he wants those who are bringing truth to the earth. After awhile of being in ministry, the enemy would exclaim to me, "There is more to life than just ministry." Which is a true statement, but little did I know he was trying to use that phrase to deter me from destiny. If he is able to detour us with distractions, then he can stop us from reaching destiny. Warfare has intensified over the past years due to the use of social media, new gadgets, also the use of drugs, alcohol, and money. My Apostle Charisse would often call it SAM; SEX, ANGER, and MONEY. According to Statista, as of 2019 over 2.77 billion people use social media daily. The enemy has used social media to trap us because it is so easy to access. Just think about how easy you grab your phone, and search for things. One of the huge traps that the devil will use to infiltrate your destiny is lust, resulting in you being bound by pornography, masturbation, and witchcraft. The enemy is a strategist, so he knows that if he can get you to participate in those actions then he can have you for his kingdom.

1 John 2:15-17

Do not love the world or the things in the world. If anyone loves the world, the love of the Father is not in him. For all that is in the world—the lust of the flesh, the lust of the eyes, and the pride of life—is not of the Father but is of the world. And the world is passing away, and the lust of it; but he who does the will of God abides forever.

To put it differently, the enemy will use what he can to get negativity and perversion into your eye-gates because it is the avenue to your soul. If he can get into your eye-gates, then it will cause a recurring memory that will enable addiction. As a prophetic vessel, take note of this because the devil doesn't want your anointing to be pure. Be mindful of the material you engage your eye-gates and ear-gates with. In today's world, there is an uprising of vulgar music. We have to watch this as young prophets. The enemy will have us listen to lyrics that get into our DNA, provoking us to speak according to the music we hear. Now I know that some of us are still young, and desire to listen to our daily music, which is not a problem. I would highly advise that you get to know yourself more, to be able to know what will alter your thinking. I have gone through a stage, where I would be moved by certain songs, causing me to desire actions and pleasures outside of the will of God. The world today has done a good job at displaying what "Living your best life" is supposed to look like. It has utilized the greed of money, sex, and control. Well, I am here to tell you that, yes we should desire to acquire money, but they fail to show you the proper way. The proper way, as in getting a job, writing business plans, and saving. On top of that, he intoxicates us with the power of sex for short-term pleasure for long term destruction. He desires for us to do things of such sort, so he can entrap us in lust. The enemy will have us blinded to the long term destruction of having children prematurely, catching diseases, or creating ungodly soul ties. Lastly, control is birthed from the spirit of pride. In this type of mindset, we act like we are always right, or that we have to always lead. Resulting in us not having a teachable spirit when the Bible tells us in **Luke 16:12** "if you be faithful in another man, who shall give you of which is your own." It is important to notice the warfare that we go through as young people, this is just some of the small things that we are up against. I was a young person that was detoured from destiny momentarily. I became in love with the satisfaction of pleasing people, wanting to belong and be accepted. I felt as though I didn't fit in, so I did whatever was necessary for me to be known. I started to develop the desire for drugs, alcohol, and the company of girls. This generated me to be blinded to my kingdom assignment on the earth because I was too distracted with temporary pleasure.

Just like me, I know that there are many young people that are going through this, and or have been through it. I thank God for having Godly Counsel around me. Although I had Godly counsel, I had ungodly counsel who loved seeing who I was in the world and these are people who don't want to see you progress forward, or who don't have the capacity to push you forward. I would advise you check your inner circle, see if these are people that will help push you to your next you. Otherwise, they could be people who are in your life only to waste your time. The enemy will insert these type of people to waste our time and slow our process down. The enemy loves magnifying situations, causing warfare in the mind, families, and personal lives. This is all to throw the vessel off course or to get you distracted. Please take note of rather you are in deep warfare or facing distraction. Warfare, in basic terms, is anything that will cause conflict to what the will of God is for your life. One of the most important fights we face while in warfare is war in the mind. The enemy comes for our minds because that is where we make decisions. If he is able to control our mind's then he can control our actions. So, the enemy will cause physiological warfare to bring confusion to God's will. God is not the author of confusion. **(1 Corinthians 14:33)** I praise God that I have learned for every demonic system, there is a prophetic strategy! That is to say for every problem the enemy tries to face you with, there is a solution. Glory be to God, I was able to find my solution through the power of prayer and having Godly counsel alongside me. I became free from the things that were holding me back from moving forward in my God-given purpose.

I want to be able to expose the plans of the enemy to free others and stop him before he gets to our next generation. Young people, please note the enemy is on assignment and wants to distract, detour, then destroy you. Some of us are facing generational curses, things that were attached to us at birth. What that means is that there were some spirits that your parents and or ancestors dealt with and have not been broken yet. You can be the catalyst in your family to break the cycles. Thank God for exposing it and DESTROYING IT NOW!! Although there are demons on assignment for us, please don't be afraid. According to **Luke 10:19** God has given us authority over ever demonic force. As we continue to live in this world please know that we are in this world, but not of this world.

Romans 12:22

And be not conformed to this world: but be ye transformed by the renewing of your mind, that ye may prove what is that good, and acceptable, and perfect, will of God.

Meaning, we do not have to do things to blend in with the world, causing unnecessary warfare. Take the time to find out what it is you are called to do and do it! As young prophets, we must stand strong, and yield no ground to the enemy! We must be destined, determined and moving forward in God's demonstration. Stand firm on the Word of God by declaring the Word of the Lord into the Earth.

Chapter 7

OFFICE OF THE PROPHET

Now that you have an understanding of some of the functions of the prophetic. We will breakdown what it means to walk in the Office of the Prophet. There is a variation between the office, the gift, and the mantle. Many prophetic vessels prophesy and think that they are either a prophet when that is not the case. Something that always resonated with me when I was being trained, is there is a certain level of warfare that comes with each different title. The Office of the Prophet requires a deeper level of intercession and even greater assignments.

Now let's go over some major prophets. Prophets are men that walk in one of the five-fold ministry, ordained by God, and not man. Prophets have a special call and are very sensitive to the spiritual realm operating in many spiritual gifts in the Bible.

Prophet Isaiah- who prophesied the coming of the Messiah Jesus Christ.

Prophet Jeremiah- who was a young prophet, his ministry started at the age of thirteen. He more than likely can relate to many of us that answer our callings at an early age. When looking at the story of Jeremiah, I was really touched because to see a young child speak the Word of the Lord with no concern of his age was powerful.

Prophet Daniel- who was brave and stood firm on the things of the Lord. These may be some prophets that I suggest to you to study to gain more information on who they were and how God used them. This will also give you more comfortability in who you were called to be.

Prophetess

Along with male prophets, there were women prophets as well, that we call prophetesses. Anna, Deborah, and Miriam were mighty women of God who moved in the vocal gifts. They spoke God's heart, also using the gifts of a demonstration by dancing and singing. I felt in my spirit that this was very imperative to share so we won't fall into the misconception that "women can't be used under the power of God." These women are living proof that it doesn't matter the gender, all God wants is a yielded vessel. He will even use animals or rocks.

A prophetess is a woman who walks in the five-fold ministry, appointed by God, not by man. She operates in the same realm as the prophet but as said before she may dance and or sing. Both prophets and prophetess are called to live a life of holiness, prayer, and fasting. This helps the vessel to stay in spiritual alignment, being in tune with the voice of God.

Exodus 15:20

And Miriam the prophetess, the sister of Aaron, took a timbrel in her hand; and all the women went out after her with timbrels and with dances.

Luke 2:36

And there was one Anna, a prophetess, the daughter of Phanuel, of the tribe of Aser: she was of a great age, and had lived with an husband seven years from her virginity;

Amos 3:7

Surely the Lord God will do nothing, but he revealeth his secret unto his servants the prophets.

Although we have the prophets and prophetesses, those outside of this five-fold ministry **(Ephesians 4:11)** should still desire to prophesy **(1 Corinthians 14:1)**. What separates the two is that the prophet should always, also have the Word of the Lord. This is because God is always speaking to us, it just depends on our sensitivity to the Spirit. Being able to discern an atmosphere, and or the spirits in operation and the ability to judge a prophetic word. You will encounter false prophets, out of season words, and or just off words and with having this ability, you're able to take the Word given before the heavens. Once taken to God, He will tell you if that was the Word of the Lord or not, with giving you instructions on how to proceed forward. As we noticed through our reading there is a difference from the Spirit of Prophecy, the Gift of Prophecy, and the Office. When the prophetic minister is going forth a lot of times they will feel the word begin to stir up or bubble up on the inside of them. This is called **NABA** (bubble up). In this realm the prophetic vessel most of the time is being stirred up by the power of the Holy Spirit or someone with spiritual authority. Whereas we know the prophet shall always hear God for himself. It is important to know the differences because too many times people take on titles without knowing the weight of responsibility. Not having the proper knowledge and training that is due with this call to the prophetic realm; has led to many misunderstandings in the Body of Christ today.

Vessels must keep "love as their standard" as Pastor Wes would say. In addition to, having integrity, humility, and prayer. Prophecy is becoming more of a normal thing in this day and time. In a sense of entertainment, or many people desiring to prophesy. This is why the power of prayer is even more important because this is where God will mold the prophet. The prophet will have no choice but to align themselves properly with the direct will of God. A lot of times we allow self-will to get in the way and go into prayer talking the whole time. Instead, we should learn to listen and allow God to respond and do what He does best. When the prophet follows biblical principles, it will help him/her to stay disciplined, humbled, and in spiritual alignment. When you follow these principles and tools you will be filled with power through prayer. It is highly important to note that the enemy doesn't want you to prevail in this area. There have been times in my spiritual walk where the enemy has tried to fight me in a place of prayer. I became distracted and too busy to pray. He would use people I love, hobbies, life circumstances, and even me to stop me from entering into the secret place. Sometimes, you must identify that the thing that is blocking you, is you. But the enemy will cause you to be blinded by putting the blame on other people to magnify the situation. If he's able to magnify the situation it will cause a bigger distraction and make you feel weakened, so you stray away from destiny. We must be able to discern the plots and plans of the enemy. I say to you, stay postured in prayer.

With this being said, the Lord placed upon my heart to expose and reiterate major spirits that prophets or prophetic vessels may face. Once again, the first ones is pride this spirit is a ruling spirit that tries to destroy the anointing. Pride loves being in control and God despises this spirit out of most. When one operates in this spirit, God cannot trust them with His secrets. Over time I have noticed that this spirit will do everything to push self, it doesn't like being in a place of crushing and humbling. It loves being in control of situations, and sometimes of people, but God has all power and control. The prophetic solution to this is staying submitted to God and his principles. If we take a look in the Bible most of the prophets were surrounded by Godly counsel, and or had an overseer. No matter how high God takes you or how many platforms you receive, stay submitted. Remember God honors those who keep covenant.

The next spirit major spirit to be mindful of, is rejection. This is a big one especially for prophetic vessels. As a prophet, God will separate you from the rest of the clique, to gain more personal time with you. It is through this time God is working on you, taking you through the process of crushing, humbling, servitude, etc. Throughout this time, it's a place of un-comfortability, the enemy uses this as a gateway to attack. Why? Well, because you are separated from certain people, but he makes you feel like you are alone. The difference between separated and alone is when you are separated, there is just a boundary that is set for detachment for a moment, or for good. Alone is when you are lonely and have absolutely no support. The enemy tries to fight you in this time, telling you that no one loves you and you aren't good enough, just any negativity. All these statements are lies and go against God's living word. It is key that you remain in prayer, also in communication with your spiritual authority during any season of separation.

The last major spirits are lust and perversion, this taints the anointing on our lives. It can stir us in the wrong direction to desire the wrong things. Lust is mainly used in the form of its sexual nature. Which means that it can encourage you to make decisions against God's standards, or your own standards. It is not only used for sexual intent, but its self seeking, greedy, mainly all about pleasure.

The spirit of perversion will have us confused and our mind's distorted about God's will. Perversion is anything that alters or twist the will of God. For example

One can be on the verge of receiving a raise on the job. But when perversion creeps in, it can alter your mind to have you think negative towards what God is trying to do. In other words it is rooted from the spirit of negativity.

Along with the hindrances listed above, there are other things to keep note of. Keep in mind "You can be anointed, but what good is your anointing if your character is not intact." This is something my mother would tell me all the time, which has helped me to stay integrable, and humble. These spirits will tear your name apart, this is because your heart isn't pure. Keep in mind that our gifts flow from our hearts. Meaning what's ever in your heart is going to come out while using your gift. This is why many times you see prophets moving in control, manipulation, hurt, sometimes fear. We have to get to a place of maturity where we yearn for the anointing, not just the gift and or talent. Many times we see people operating out of gifting but no anointing. It is easy to do something you are good at, but the anointing cost. You have to be willing to pay for the fire of God to flow through you. Remain pure and alert of the distinctive spirits that try to destroy the prophet.

Chapter 8

FALSE PROPHETS

DEUTERONOMY 18:20

But the prophet, which shall presume to speak a word in my name, which I have not commanded him to speak, or that shall speak in the name of other gods, even that prophet shall die.

MARK 13:22

For false Christs and false prophets shall rise, and shall shew signs and wonders, to seduce, if it were possible, even the elect.

Lastly, we will discuss false prophets and their characteristics. Another word used when discussing false prophets is, Ziyd. **Ziyd** means to cook up or boil up. Most of the time, false prophets operate in those exact spirits that we just discussed in previous chapters. They move in pride, manipulation, jealousy, envy, error, and fear. These are some ways that you can identify false prophets, although there are some character traits they always won't expose themselves in that way. Two of the main ways a false prophet operates is in deception and error. They are good at hiding themselves trying to blend in with the true prophets, that's why discernment is needed. They will tell you things that go against the Word of God as I said they are smart in their ways. Just as we use God to be our source, the kingdom of darkness uses their source, Satan. Over the years of ministry I've noticed that some people function under the wrong source. Unfortunately, depending on how deep they are into it, they can give someone an accurate word just as a prophet could. **1 Corinthians 14:33**, and **Psalms 10:4** describes it is possible to access a different source other than God. False prophets move in the spirit of error, which means they try to twist the Word of God. Nowadays there are psychics, sorcerers, medians, sue sayers, and much more. Not to mention blind witching, where someone is being controlled by a witching spirit and has no idea. We have to go this deep and expose so we won't be misled.

Many are being controlled and manipulated by these spirits and it results in us becoming stagnant in our God-given purpose. Some may notice, but there still is a fear to pull away. A lot of times when these spirits are in operation they drain others out for personal gain, giving themselves more power. In the end, you feel like you are stuck and can't move forward spiritually, and emotionally. The way they get you is by natural things to get you to follow them gaining your trust. What I mean by that is it may seem like you are gaining materialistic things, but be mindful that it's a tool to trap you. Then when you are trying to be set free it's hard to escape.

Be aware that these spirits operate out of familiar spirits, and divination. Put in another way they prophesy to people based on what they feel, sense or know, covering their deceitful ways by attaching God's name on it. When in reality it is not the power of God in operation but the kingdom of darkness. Glory be to God, He has given us power over every demonic force. We should have nothing to fear but should discern people and ask God why they are in our lives. Every prophet must have their left-hand ministry together, this means they are living a lifestyle of holiness behind closed doors. I have observed that we as the body of Christ love prophecy, especially accurate vessels. But we allow ourselves to get caught up on the prophet and not what was prophesied. Ultimately, we miss what God is trying to say, which puts us in a position to where now we chase prophecy. All this to say, something I learned from a wise man of God, "you have to be mindful on who you let speak into your life, and impart into you."

We have no time to be chasing down a prophet or becoming a prophecy junky, where you just have collected word upon word. There will be no shift in our lives, until you do what God has told you to do. I have to explain this so that we know that just because someone gives you an accurate word, doesn't mean you have to submit and follow them. I've seen this happen, and in too many cases people's lives are put in jeopardy. If you go back to the previous chapter, we talked a little about judging the word. Tape every word you get, take it before God ask if this is what He's saying for your life, then ask him to reveal the heart of the prophet. As a prophet of God, I want to tell you this, every single word that's spoken into your life should be backed up by the Word of God.

The Word of God is all truth, and anything contrary is sent to deceive God's people. False prophets like to cook up and conjure up a word speaking their own heart or own desires. , They will use everyday precepts to give a "word". Through the *Liquid Fire School of the Prophetic Training*, we learn there are **two types** of false prophets:

The prophet who is speaking in the name of the Lord falsely, speaking lies presumably. Then there are the false prophets who speak in the name of other gods (**Jeremiah 23:16** and **Isaiah 29:13**).

Another way to identify these prophets is by the fruit that they bear (**Matthew 7:17**) Look at their actions and appetite (the things they hunger for and desire) because there will be signs of ungodliness in their lives. You will be able to tell a good tree from a bad, by the fruit it bears. We as prophetic vessels must continue to rise because we are living in a time where false prophets are speaking boldly, **Matthew 24:11**. We must be in position and knowledgeable to expose them.

Below here are some character traits

• False prophets speak false prophecies.

• False prophets bring forth evil fruit.

• False prophets speak in the name of other gods.

• False prophets speak falsely in the Name of the Lord.

• False prophets personal lives do not line up with the Word of God.

- False prophets speak words that lack Dunamis power to bring to past the content of the words.

- False prophets idolize money.

- False prophets lack self-control.

- False prophets have ungodly desires.

- False prophets are frivolous and light.

- False prophets are liars.

- False prophets prophesy false revelation.

- False prophets make plans to deceive others.

If you recognize that you have any of these characteristics, seek Godly counsel.

Proverbs 11:4

Where no counsel is the people fall: but in the multitude of counsellors there is safety.

Prophetic Declaration

As a young Prophet it is important to understand the power of the decisions that you make in your youth. These decisions can have the ability to dis-pattern or distract you or they can catapult and increase you in the prophetic mandate that's upon your life. Therefore, you must press pass any opposition that the world brings.

I decree and declare that you as a prophet in your youth will be strong and courageous you will not falter concerning your kingdom mandate. I decree and declare that you will have the knowledge and revelation beyond your years. I thank you Father for apostolic shifting in the mind of the prophet, I decree and declare that new prophetic rivers will open up on the inside of you. Father I ask that the heart of the young prophet would be covered as they grow and that he/she will guard their hearts from seeds of rejection, hurt, disappointment, and pain. I decree and declare that you would anoint the voice of the vessels that read this book to be a trumpet in their cities, their states, and in this nation. I thank you God that you will give them divine friendships and relationships. I thank you God for Apostolic Fathers and leaders that will mentor the next generation of prophets. I speak a fresh new wind of anointing to be upon your confidence and identity in who God has called for you to be. You will not be pushed to bypass your process for platforms or financial gain. I declare and decree that you will not walk with the spirit of fear but **2 Timothy 1:7** will cover you. I pray that the loins of the next generation of Prophets shall be girded with truth. I speak a mantle of integrity and humility to be a cloak upon the prophetic vessel.I declare and decree a consuming fire to burn out anything that's not like God. I thank you for being a blue flame that will burn internally on the inside of the prophet. Father, I thank you for every prophet that will move in the spiritual gifts to win their generation to the Kingdom. Lord allow these words to be bound to their heart in Jesus Name.

Love,

Prophetess Shauntae Warren

Prophetic Prayer

Father in the Name of Jesus,

We come to you humble in our spirits asking that you forgive us for sins of commission & omission. Sin that we know, and sin that we don't know. Any thought any action or deed, that has been displeasing to you that will cause our prayers to be hindered. We pray that in this season and time as you pour out your spirit, that the young shall prophesy with accuracy and integrity while displaying Godly character. Father in the name of Jesus, you said in your word according to Acts 2:17 "And it shall come to pass in the last days, saith God that I will pour my spirit upon all flesh and your sons and daughters shall prophesy, and your young men shall see visions, and the old shall dream dreams". We bind every trick, snare, plot, scheme and plan of the enemy. That will try to distract, displace, and discourage and or destroy us. We bind our feet to the will of God, that we may walk in obedience, humility, and patience. We thank God for his grace as we continue to deliver the word of the lord with fire. That as we speak, the word would go spirit to spirit and burn anything that's not like you God. We release new prophetic mantels and apostolic structure as all things are done decently and in order. Father, you said in your word according to **1 Corinthians 14:1** "Follow after charity and desire spiritual gifts, but rather that ye may prophesy."Therefore we pray that young prophets will pursue love, that love will be the standard as our gifts flow through our heart. We pray that you heal every area of hurt, disappointment, and un-forgiveness. We remove every spirit of rejection, bitterness, and depression in Jesus name. We thank you that the gifts on the inside of them will come forth with purified fire. Father we ask that young prophets will stay in divine alignment with your mandate for their lives. That you will get the glory as people experience victory.

In Jesus name we pray

Amen!

Pastor Wes Warren

Sr. Pastor Elohim Kingdom Ministries

Prayer of Redemption

Father in the Name of Jesus, I desire a greater relationship with you. Draw me closer to you, help me to understand who you are in my life. I want to know you as my personal savior, in Jesus' Name.

The Bible declares, according to **Romans 10:9**, "That if thou shalt confess with thy mouth the Lord Jesus, and shalt believe in thine heart that God hath raised him from the dead, thou shalt be saved." If you make this confession right now, you will be saved.

Reader, you may be young or you may be mature, and as you were reading this book you began to desire a closer relationship with God. I recommend that you find a place of worship that will teach you Kingdom Principles. We pray this prayer will ignite your passion for God!

Contact Page

Prophet Weshaun Warren is available for speaking engagements, seminars, prayer, conferences, and book signings.

For booking please contact:

ELOHIM KINGDOM MINISTRIES:

Phone Number: (743) 334-8796

Phone Number: (734) 833-7819

Email: Elohimkministries@gmail.com

Facebook: Weshaun Warren or Elohim Kingdom ministries

www.ingramcontent.com/pod-product-compliance
Lightning Source LLC
Chambersburg PA
CBHW020515030426
42337CB00011B/394